MATERIAL WORLD

CHANGING MATERIALS

Robert Snedden

Heinemann
LIBRARY

www.heinemann.co.uk/library

Visit our website to find out more information about Heinemann Library books.

To order:

☎ Phone 44 (0) 1865 888066

🖹 Send a fax to 44 (0) 1865 314091

💻 Visit the Heinemann Bookshop at www.heinemann.co.uk/library to browse our catalogue and order online.

First published in Great Britain by Heinemann Library, Halley Court, Jordan Hill, Oxford OX2 8EJ, part of Harcourt Education. Heinemann is a registered trademark of Harcourt Education Ltd.

Editorial: Nancy Dickmann
Design: Victoria Bevan and Q2A
Picture research: Mica Brancic
Production: Julie Carter and Alison Parsons

Origination: Chroma Graphics
Printed and bound in China by South China Printing Co. Ltd.

13-digit ISBN 978 0 431 12150 5

12 11 10 09 08
10 9 8 7 6 5 4 3 2 1

British Library Cataloguing in Publication Data
Snedden, Robert
Changing Materials. – (Material World) - 2nd ed.
1. Matter – Properties – Juvenile literature
2. Materials science – Juvenile literature
I. Title
530.4
A full catalogue record for this book is available from the British Library.

Acknowledgements
The publishers would like to thank the following for permission to reproduce photographs:
Actionplus p. **5** (P Millereau); Environmental Images p. **16** (Vanessa Miles); Environmental Picture Library pp. **19** (Pete Addis), **7**, **24** (Leslie Garland); Network p. **21** (Barry Lewis); Photolibrary p. **26**; Sally and Richard Greenhill, p. **20**; Science Photo Library pp. **4** (Martin Bond); **10** (Charles D Winters), **11** (Rosenfeld Images Ltd), **12** (John Greim), **18**; Tony Stone Images pp. **8** (David Hoffman), **22** (Christopher Bissell), **23** (Robert Yager), **29** (Matthew McVay).

Cover photograph of molten metal being poured from a crucible reproduced with permission of Getty Images/Stone/Thomas Lindley.

Contents

Some words are shown in bold, **like this**. You can find out what they mean by looking in the Glossary.

A world of change

None of the objects around us remain unchanged over time. You will have seen how things get broken, batteries go dead, clothes wear out and food goes bad. These materials and all the other materials that we use are acted upon by many outside forces.

Many of the materials we use are thrown away after being used for only a short time.

The right choice

Some materials are designed to be used just once, such as the tissue paper you use for blowing your nose on. Others materials have to last longer. It would be incredibly wasteful and expensive to have to buy a new set of clothes every day, which rules out the use of tissue paper for clothing! When a materials scientist sets out to choose a material for a particular purpose, knowing the conditions that the material is likely to meet is vital.

Chemical changes

There are few materials that do not react in some way with their environment. Coming into contact with other materials can cause chemical changes to take place. For example, iron rusts if it comes into contact with the air, and so has to be protected. Kitchen utensils have to be made from materials that will not react with the foods they touch. A car battery has to be made of a material that can withstand the **acid** it contains. A materials scientist has to know the chemical characteristics of a material in order to know how it will react with the other materials it could meet during everyday use.

Physical forces

The materials we use are affected by physical forces too, such as changes in temperature, stresses and pressure changes. The extent of these forces depends on the job a material has to do.

Raw materials

Knowing how materials react to change is not only important to the way they are used but also to the way in which they are manufactured or obtained from **raw materials**. For example, plastics and glass are made from chemicals and moulded into shape; metals have to be extracted from **ores**. Materials scientists are always looking for ways to make new and improved materials. Understanding how they change is fundamental to that search.

A glass bicycle might look wonderful, but what would happen the first time it hit a bump? A new material will be given a series of tests to make sure that it can perform the job it is needed for.

Chemical reactions

A **chemical reaction** takes place when two or more substances react together to form new substances. Chemical reactions are different from the physical changes that can take place in a material. In a physical change, such as melting or freezing, the **atoms** making up the substance are still joined together in the same way, whether it is a solid, liquid or gas.

When two substances react together the bonds that hold the atoms together are broken and reformed to make new substances.

Breaking the bonds

For a chemical reaction to take place the **bonds** that hold atoms together have to be broken and reformed in a different way. Chemical reactions can be slow, such as when iron combines with oxygen to form rust, or very fast, as in an explosion. Most chemical reactions produce heat, although some need heat to get them started.

Chemical equations

When a chemical reaction takes place it seems that one substance has disappeared to be replaced by a new substance. Although the new substance might look totally different, the total number of atoms present does not change. In a chemical reaction matter is neither created nor destroyed. Chemists use chemical equations to set out what occurs in chemical reactions.

For example, a chemist would write down rusting like this:

$$4Fe + 3O_2 = 2Fe_2O_3$$
iron + oxygen = iron oxide (rust)

The equation shows how iron reacts with oxygen gas to form solid rust. The chemical formula for rust is Fe_2O_3. A chemical formula is simply a group of letters and numbers that tells us how many atoms of each **element** are combined in a **compound**. What it means in this case is that four atoms of iron (Fe) combine with three **molecules** of oxygen (each made up of two oxygen atoms) to form two molecules of iron oxide, the chemical name for rust.

If iron is left exposed to the air it will react with oxygen to form iron oxide, or rust. Covering it with a protective coat can help to prevent this happening.

The substances on the left of the equation are called the reactants. The reactants are the substances that take part in a chemical reaction, in other words, they are the ones that are changed. Chemists have worked out the proportions of atoms involved in chemical reactions by carefully measuring the amounts of each reactant involved. You can see that there are ten atoms in total (four iron and six oxygen). The material on the right of the equation is called the product. It is the result of the reaction. Some reactions have more than one product. In this case there is one product, rust. Add up the atoms on the right and you will see that the product also contains ten atoms, as there are two molecules of iron oxide, each made up of two iron atoms and three oxygen atoms.

Reaction rates

It is important to know how materials will react when they are brought together. Some chemicals can react together very rapidly producing a great deal of energy and this could be dangerous if it happened unexpectedly.

An explosion takes place as a result of a very rapid and highly energetic chemical reaction.

Chemical kinetics

The branch of chemistry that investigates the rates of chemical reactions is called chemical kinetics. The word 'kinetic' means moving. **Kinetic energy** is energy of movement. In order for chemicals to react together the molecules that make them up have to be on the move so they can collide with each other. If the molecules bang together with enough force the bonds holding them together can be broken and reformed to make new compounds. The atoms in a solid move much less than those in a liquid or a gas – they just vibrate while staying in the same position. In a reaction such as rusting, which involves a solid, collisions with enough energy don't happen very often and so the iron rusts slowly.

Changing the rate

There are various ways in which the rate of a reaction can be changed. Heating the chemicals involved in the reaction gives the molecules more kinetic energy and so increases the chances of collisions taking place. On the other hand, cooling the reactants slows down the movement of the molecules, so cutting down on the number of collisions. This is why freezing food is a good way of preventing it from going bad.

The size of the particles involved in the reaction is also important. A reaction can only take place if the reactants come into contact. A large lump of coal will burn fairly slowly and steadily because only the surface of the coal is in contact with the oxygen in the air. If that same lump is ground down into powder it will explode violently if it is blown into a flame. The reason for this is that the total surface area of the fine particles is much greater than the surface area of the original lump. This means that there is a much larger area over which the reaction can take place.

TRY IT YOURSELF

You will need:

sand

water

vinegar

bicarbonate of soda

red food-colouring

large dish

small plastic bottle

I   **Add some food colouring to the vinegar.**

2   **Fill the bottle halfway up with water and dissolve a couple of teaspoons of bicarbonate of soda in it.**

3   **Pile sand around the bottle to make a volcano cone, leaving the top of the bottle uncovered. Now pour the red vinegar into the bottle and watch your volcano erupt!**

Oxidation and reduction

Oxidation is a chemical reaction in which a substance combines with oxygen. When you burn something oxidation is taking place very rapidly. When iron rusts oxidation is taking place slowly as the iron combines with oxygen from the air. Inside your body the food you eat is combined with the air you breathe to produce carbon dioxide, water and energy. This is another example of oxidation.

Chemists have now discovered that some reactions of this type can take place without oxygen. So oxidation can be described more generally as a reaction in which atoms lose **electrons**.

A breathalyser is used by police to determine how much alcohol someone has consumed. Alcohol causes an oxidation reaction to take place that makes a chemical in the breathalyser change colour.

Redox reactions

The electrons released during oxidation don't just fly off and disappear, they are captured by another substance. This process, by which atoms of an element gain electrons, is called **reduction**. Oxidation and reduction always happen together in a balanced reaction, called a **redox reaction**.

When powdered iron is heated with copper oxide the copper oxide is reduced to copper metal and the iron is oxidised to iron oxide.

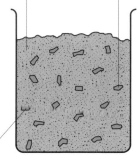

Iron + copper(II) oxide   →   Iron(II) oxide + copper

Black copper oxide

Heat to start reaction

Pinkish copper metal

Reduction was originally used to describe any chemical reaction in which a substance either combines with hydrogen or loses oxygen.

When iron ore, a compound of iron and oxygen, is heated with carbon, the carbon acts as a reducing agent. A reducing agent is a substance that removes oxygen or donates (gives) electrons. The carbon removes the oxygen from the iron ore, leaving iron behind. The carbon is oxidized and becomes carbon dioxide gas.

Combustion
Combustion is a chemical reaction that usually involves the rapid combination of oxygen with a fuel, producing energy in the form of heat and light. This energy is called the heat of combustion. The fuel may take the form of a solid, liquid or gas. Combustion occurs, for example, when petrol **vapour** is ignited in a combustion engine – the energy produced is used to move a car. The lowest temperature at which a solid or liquid will catch fire is called its ignition temperature. The ignition temperature and heat of combustion differ from one fuel to another.

Acids

Acids are found in all sorts of places – in fizzy drinks, car batteries and even in our stomachs. Many acids occur naturally. Hydrochloric acid is produced in your stomach to help digest food. Acids are also widely used in the production of food and drinks, and as preservatives to kill bacteria in food. However, many are poisonous, and strong acids such as sulphuric acid are highly corrosive, which means that they can burn clothes or skin. Acids in rain can damage buildings and kill trees. The chemical industry produces 150 million tonnes of corrosive sulphuric acid a year – it is an essential part of the production of fertilizers, paints, detergents and other materials.

Acid properties

An acid is one of a group of chemical compounds which have certain properties in common. Acids can dissolve many metals. Solutions of acids have a sour taste and produce a burning sensation if they come into contact with the skin.

Acid rain causes a great deal of damage to stone. Some carvings that had lasted for hundreds of years have been severely eroded by acid rain.

An acid is defined by chemists as a compound that dissolves in water to produce hydrogen **ions** in solution. The strength of an acid depends on how readily it breaks up in solution to form hydrogen ions. For example, when it is dissolved in water every molecule of hydrogen chloride releases a hydrogen ion to form hydrochloric acid. Hydrochloric acid is therefore considered to be a strong acid. Acetic acid, one of the ingredients of vinegar, is a weak acid. It produces only a few hydrogen ions in solution.

Litmus is used as an indicator to test whether liquids are acid or **alkaline**. Litmus is a dye obtained from various lichens. Blue litmus paper will turn red if it is brought into contact with acid.

0	Battery acid
1	
2	Lemon juice
3	Cola
4	Tomato juice
5	Black coffee
6	Rain water
	Milk
7	Distilled water
8	Sea water
9	Baking soda
10	Soap
11	Milk of magnesia
12	
13	Caustic soda
14	

Increasing acidity

Increasing alkalinity

This scale shows some common materials and their pHs.

Inorganic and organic acids

Generally, inorganic acids do not contain carbon atoms. Many inorganic acids are strong acids and can be highly corrosive. They are used in the production of other chemicals and in the refining of crude oil. Sulphuric acid, a strong inorganic acid, is commonly used in car batteries. Other important inorganic acids are hydrochloric acid and nitric acid.

Organic acids are always carbon compounds. They are used in drinks, cosmetics, medicines and soaps. The first known acid was vinegar, an organic acid. Common organic acids include citric acid, which is found in citrus fruits, and ascorbic acid, or vitamin C.

Physical changes

As we have seen, materials are changed by chemical reactions. One material reacts with another and the atoms that make them up are rearranged to form something new. On the whole, however, when we use materials we are interested just as much in their physical properties as in their chemical properties. The way in which materials are affected by changes in temperature, in pressure and by bending and stretching and other forces determines how they are used.

Ice cream only stays semi-solid while it is cold. On a hot day it will soon melt and drip if you don't eat it quickly!

Physical properties

Here are just a few examples of how a material's physical properties allow it to be used for different purposes. Glass is very brittle but it is useful because it is transparent and it can be moulded into different shapes when it is molten. Plastics are easy to mould into a limitless variety of shapes. They are lightweight and waterproof, and so make ideal containers, although they have the disadvantage of being resistant to chemical attack so they do not break down when discarded. Metals are tough and strong, easily shaped into thin wires or into sheets, good conductors of electricity and heat and highly reflective when polished. All these physical characteristics make metals very useful materials indeed.

If a solution of salt in water is allowed to evaporate deposits of salt crystals are left behind.

Solubility

Many substances can be dissolved in water, or some other liquids, to form a solution. These substances are said to be **soluble**. Salt can be dissolved in water to give a liquid solution of salt and water, for example. Although the salt may no longer be visible it has not been changed chemically. Dissolving a substance is a physical change. If the water is removed by **evaporation** a solid deposit of salt will be left behind.

TRY IT YOURSELF

You will need:
a shallow dish
a beaker
some warm water
table salt

1 Pour the water into the beaker and add salt, stirring until it has dissolved.
2 Pour some of the salt solution into a shallow dish and leave it in a warm place until the water has **evaporated**.

You will see the salt crystals that have been left behind. Taste a little to prove to yourself that the salt has not been changed by dissolving in the water.

Temperature changes

Materials are often exposed to heat. We use heat to cook our food and to warm our homes. In industry, heat is used to refine crude oil and to separate metals from their ores. Heat is also used to melt materials so that they can be reshaped. Changes in temperature can have many effects on different materials. Metals expand when they get hot and **contract** when they cool.

Railway engineers were aware that metals expanded on hot days, so rail tracks were laid with gaps to allow for this.

Temperature and energy

All materials are made up of atoms or molecules and these are always moving. If they are moving slowly, the material is said to have a low level of **internal energy**. If they are moving rapidly, it has a high level of internal energy. Hot materials have high internal energy levels, cold materials have low levels. Temperature is a measurement of internal energy levels. If a material with a high level of energy comes into contact with a material that has a low level, internal energy passes from high to low until the temperature of both materials is the same. This passage of energy from one object to another is called heat.

The water in a hot bath has a high level of internal energy. If you step into it, it makes you feel warm as heat is transferred to your cooler body. However, if you step into a cold bath your body will have a higher internal energy and heat will flow from you to the bathwater, making you feel rather chilly!

Expanding and contracting

When heat flows into a material the atoms or molecules take up more space as they move more rapidly and the substance expands. The opposite happens when heat flows out of a material. A thermometer indicates temperature change according to how much the mercury inside it expands and contracts as it heats up or cools down.

Moving heat

Heat moves through a material by **conduction**. If a metal rod is heated at one end, for example, the atoms in the hot end begin to move faster as their internal energy increases. These atoms move faster and strike atoms further along the rod. In this way, the heat travels from atom to atom through the metal.

If the heated metal rod heats the air around it the heated air expands and rises and cooler air replaces it. The cooler air that is now near the rod becomes warm and rises in its turn. This flow of heated air moving away from a hot object and cooler air flowing towards it is called a **convection current**. Convection currents carry heat through liquids as well as gases.

Insulating materials

Heat does not travel easily through some materials by conduction. These materials, such as plastic and wood, are called insulators. This is why many cooking utensils have plastic or wood handles. The metal part of the utensil heats rapidly but the handle stays cool, protecting your hand.

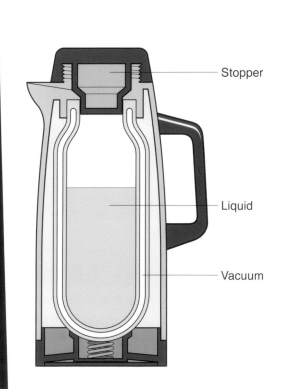

Stopper

Liquid

Vacuum

A vacuum flask has a vacuum held between two layers to prevent heat being conducted in or out.

Radioactivity

Some materials are composed of atoms that are unstable. Over time the atoms break up and become other chemical elements. Materials that do this are said to be **radioactive**. The energy produced as these materials decay can be put to use in nuclear power stations and batteries for pacemakers. Radioactive substances change, or decay, at a known rate, so we can work out how old a sample is – for example, radioactive carbon dating is used to tell us how old archaeological specimens are.

What is radioactivity?

Atoms are made up of clouds of negatively charged electrons surrounding a heavier, positively charged **nucleus**. The nucleus of every element except hydrogen consists of particles called **protons** and **neutrons**. A normal hydrogen nucleus has just a single proton. Any change in the number of protons in the nucleus produces an atom of a different element. Radioactive substances, such as the elements radium, uranium and plutonium, have very large nuclei and are unstable. They release **radiation** to take on a more stable form. The process of giving off atomic particles is called radioactive decay. As radioactive elements decay, they change into different forms of the same element or into other elements, until finally they reach a point at which they are stable and nonradioactive.

Uranium 238 loses an alpha particle and becomes thorium

Through several more steps the thorium breaks down to radium 226

In the course of a lengthy many-step process radioactive uranium eventually becomes stable.

The breakdown continues until the atom becomes a stable form of lead

Half-lives

The rate of radioactive decay is measured in half-lives. That is the time it takes for one half of the atoms in the radioactive material to decay. This takes place at different rates in different elements or different forms of the same element. Half-lives range from fractions of a second to billions of years.

Particle radiation

When the nucleus of a radioactive element breaks down it can emit radioactivity in a number of different ways. Particle radiation consists of protons, neutrons, and electrons. Alpha particles are fast-moving groups of two protons and two neutrons and are identical to the nuclei of helium atoms. They do not travel far and can easily be stopped by a sheet of paper. Most alpha particles eventually become atoms of helium gas. Beta particles are electrons. They are also fast moving and can travel further than alpha particles. A thin sheet of metal will stop them. Gamma rays are not particles but a form of high-energy electromagnetic radiation. They are much more difficult to stop and a thick sheet of lead is needed to block them.

Artificial radioactive substances are made by exploding nuclear weapons and in nuclear reactors. These new radioactive atoms are called fission products. Used fuel from nuclear power plants contains many fission products, such as plutonium 239 and barium 140. This used fuel, called nuclear waste, remains hazardous for thousands of years.

The problem of what to do with dangerous nuclear waste has never been satisfactorily solved.